BECAUSE I'M SAVED

YOUR NEXT STEP TO BEGIN A CLOSER WALK WITH CHRIST

JIM BAIZE

BECAUSE I'M SAVED

By Jim W. Baize

Copyright 2018 by Jim W. Baize

Published by Faithway Publishers LLC
Springfield, MO 65807

Faithway Publishers is a publishing house dedicated to publishing books with high family values. We believe the vision for Faithway Publishers is to provide families and individuals with user-friendly materials that will help them in their daily lives and experiences.

It is our hope that this book will help you discover truths for your own life and help you meet the needs of others. May you be richly blessed.

All rights reserved. No part of this book may be used or reproduced in any manner whatsoever or stored in any database or retrieval system without written permission except in the case of brief quotations used in critical articles and reviews. Requests for permissions should be addressed to:

Faithway Publishers
2131 W. Republic Rd. PMB 211
Springfield, MO 65807
417-889-4803
www.faithwaypublishers.com

Editor: Gail Ledbetter
Cover Design: Lee Fredrickson
Interior design: Keith Bennett
ISBN: 978-1-947828-04-9
Printed in the United States of America

CONTENTS

INTRODUCTION 5

LESSON ONE - Baptism 7

LESSON TWO - The Local Church 11

LESSON THREE - Stewardship 15

LESSON FOUR - Witnessing 19

LESSON FIVE - Prayer & Bible Reading 23

LESSON SIX - Problems 27

SPIRITUAL GROWTH CHART 30

LESSON SEVEN - The Holy Spirit 31

19 REASONS - Why A Christian Cannot Be Lost 35

INTRODUCTION

I recently read the startling account of a young woman giving birth to a baby girl in the restroom of a college library. This is unusual in itself, yet the really shocking part of the story is that after the baby had been born without any medical assistance at all, in such adverse conditions, the mother left the newborn child to the mercy of her new surroundings and to whomever would hopefully find and take care of her. I was appalled at the terrible lack of love and attention exhibited by the young woman. And yet, as a preacher very much concerned about soul winning and "reproducing" disciples, how many times have I left new converts, babes in Christ, to the mercy of the world, cults, and the devil? Our intentions are good. We want to see folks born anew, but our follow-up must be better, and we must combat "spiritual infant mortality."

Thus, I am prayerfully writing this Bible study booklet to help ground and grow new Christians. If you have just received Christ, you have made the greatest decision a person can make in this life; however, it does not end here. This is just the beginning. Jesus Christ has just given you eternal life with Him, but He wants to give you an "abundant life" now and until He returns or until you are taken home. You may help Him by giving yourself wholly to Him. This is your reasonable service (Romans 12:1-2). The Christian walk is a practical walk. It is one you can put on in the morning when you rise from bed. It wears well at the breakfast table with the family. It is appropriate in your place of business, in school or at any social function. It will not wear out, nor will it become obsolete. Therefore, take it with you wherever you go. Make it work for you. It is exciting, fulfilling, energizing, and satisfying. Most of all, it is available. In fact, if the Holy Spirit had His way in our lives, victorious living would be the norm for every born-again Christian. We call ourselves "Christians," now let us live out our professions. May God bless us as we learn from Him. If I can be of any service to you, I would consider it a privilege.

BEGIN A CLOSER WALK WITH CHRIST

LESSON 1

Water, Water, Everywhere...

Baptism

One of the most controversial subjects in Christendom is the ordinance of baptism. An ordinance is simply something that God has ordained, instituted or decreed. Some faiths call it a sacrament and define baptism as an act that is sacred and efficacious (or necessary) for salvation. As New Testament Christians, we do not believe water saves the soul. Only that which Christ has done on the cross of Calvary can make atonement for our sins. Some say that the blood meets the water in the baptistry, and this saves the sinner. If you mix blood with water, the result is diluted blood. If you mix your good works with the blood of Jesus, you have diluted (and deluded) the Gospel.

There are many Scriptures that deal with the topic of baptism, and we believe that there are none that teach that baptism saves us! (Acts 2:38; Ephesians 5:26; 1 Peter 3:20; Mark 16:16; Ephesians 2:3-9; Galatians 2:16; Rom. 1:17; Romans 3:28; Romans 4:16). We believe that a complete study of the Scriptures will in no way lead one to believe that we must be baptized by water so that our sins might be forgiven. In fact, in I Corinthians 1:14, the Apostle Paul states, "I thank God that I baptized none of you but Crispus and Gaius." He continues in vs. 17, "For Christ sent me not to baptize, but to preach the gospel..." Truly this would be a remarkable statement if baptism were necessary for salvation. Why would Paul pride himself in the fact that he did not baptize if salvation is dependent on it? The Scriptures further reveal that Jesus, Himself, did not baptize, but His disciples took care of this ordinance for Him (see John 4:1-2). The attempt to place Christians under the bondage of law prompted the writings of both Galatians and Colossians. Paul makes it clear that salvation is in no way dependent on any works we do (Ephesians 2:8-9). In fact, if we add anything to grace, we destroy the very concept of free salvation, and then Christ has died in vain (Galatians 2:21)! Please know, we do not downplay the importance of baptism in its dual symbolic form. Baptism symbolizes both the death, burial, and resurrection of Christ, and the death and burial of the old life and the resurrection to a new life for a child of God. However, do not fall into doctrinal error by declaring it is helping to "earn" part of your salvation! May I hasten to say, we believe in baptism. The Great Commission, given by Jesus Christ Himself, commands us to baptize believers. That is why when a person receives Christ as his Savior, he should also be willing to follow Him in Christian baptism. (Matthew 10:32; Matthew 28:18-20; Acts 2:41). A person becomes a soldier when he takes the oath. Later, he receives a uniform that identifies him as a member of the U.S. Army. In much the same way, salvation is a personal and private experience which ought to be made public and shared with others in believers' baptism. Let everyone know you are in the Lord's Army.

Baptism is an ordinance of the local church. Three things are necessary for scriptural baptism:

1. **The proper candidate is necessary.** A born-again Christian is the only person ever baptized in the Bible. Notice in the Word of God that babies are never baptized. If you were baptized before your actual salvation experience, then you were not really baptized. You merely got wet! Now you need to consent to believers' baptism.

2. **The proper method is necessary.** The meaning of "baptize" is to plunge, dip or immerse. Nowhere in the Word of God is anyone ever baptized by sprinkling.

3. **The proper administrator is necessary.** This is a person with the authority of a local, New Testament, Gospel-preaching church.

Baptism is our identification with Christ (Romans 6:4). We are, in effect, burying the "old man" and rising to walk in "newness" of life. We are showing forth the truth of the Gospel by picturing Christ's death, burial, and resurrection. It is one of the first steps in our public profession of Him.

Therefore, after you have received Christ, follow Him in baptism. But be careful that your baptism is according to the whole tenor of Scripture.

1. Who may be baptized? *Acts 2:41; Acts 8:36-37*

2. Why should you be baptized? *Matthew 10:32*

3. Does your baptism save you? *Ephesians 2:8-9; 1 Peter 3:21* (note the word "figure" or symbol.)

4. If baptism could save you, why didn't Jesus and Paul baptize? *I Corinthians 1:14, 17; John 4:2*

5. Does just anyone have the proper authority to baptize?

6. Does the Bible anywhere teach the baptism of babies?

7. Have you been scripturally baptized? If not, will you be?

If the answer to this last question is "yes," congratulations! You have taken the first step of obedience in the Christian endeavor. But, don't stop now! This is only the beginning.

BEGIN A CLOSER WALK WITH CHRIST

LESSON 2

Here's the Church, Here's the Steeple, Look Inside...

The Local Church

The Bible tells us that Christ, "loved the church and gave Himself for it" (Ephesians 5:25). There are those today who believe the church is outdated and unnecessary. Perhaps their church is—but Christ's church is not! Everything of lasting value revolves around local, New Testament churches.

If the local churches of America closed their doors, most missionaries would have to come home. If the local churches of America folded up, city-wide evangelistic meetings would not have the organization, prayer, financial support, and workers that they have now. If it were not for the local churches, Christianity would be routed and reversed in short order.

Gospel churches also have been maligned by "super saints" who claim they will have nothing to do with organized religion. (One wonders if they prefer unorganized religion!) Actually, the word "religion" is somewhat suspect. Paul referred to the Athenians as being "too religious" but still lost. "Christianity" is a more accurate term than "religion," for it specifies a unique religion—unique to Jesus Christ. Attacks upon the churches of Jesus Christ are attacks upon Christ Himself because He instituted them. One is reminded of the carnal Christians of I Corinthians, who claimed to be the most spiritual by stating, "We are of Christ...." Churches ought to be independent (not controlled as to policy, doctrine or polity by any outside person or group apart from the local congregation, pastor, and God Himself). Fellowships or denominations permit churches to interact and are healthful and beneficial for encouragement, edification, and for the sponsoring of new baby churches, missionary outreaches, etc. They should in no way dictate policies. The church is pictured as the "bride of Christ" (Ephesians 5:23), and certainly, it is in a beloved position to our Lord. A bride is always very important to the groom! We believe in the "body of Christ." We also believe in local New Testament churches proclaiming the Gospel here and around the world. You can be a Christian without being a church member, but you will never be a successful Christian apart from a vital local church ministry. Be careful to find a church that will provide you with spiritual nourishment and basic training. Not all churches, sad to say, are doing the job today. Find one that is. Some are dead. They may be orthodox (straight and sound in belief), but dead.

There are also the liberal "new theology" churches. These churches have discarded scriptural absolutes for expediency. Their standards vary with the whims of the populace, and they subscribe to "situational ethics." Those who follow situational ethics say it may be alright to steal in certain circumstances, etc. They have the "form of godliness, but deny the power thereof." So many new converts really wrestle with the traditions of men and of churches.

Just recently, I visited a lady who had received Jesus Christ as her personal Savior. She had attended our church three weeks in a row and really enjoyed it and felt "fed." Her children also enjoyed the teaching in our Sunday School departments. Guess what her biggest problem was? She had been taught works for salvation from birth, and as the Bible was preached, conflicts kept surfacing. Traditions (like praying to saints) from her former church had such a strong pull that they almost rode rough-shod over the plain truth of the Word of God! Only you, who have been there, fully appreciate what I'm saying. I'm convinced that if Jesus Himself were to preach to her, she would have initial pangs within as He taught certain truths!

People of God, let's be people of the Book! If the Bible says it – believe it. If men or churches say it, examine it juxtaposed to the Bible. For example, people believe in infant baptism, but why? Not one instance of infant baptism is recorded in the Bible!

People insist there were three wise men. Why? Nowhere in the Bible is it recorded that there were three wise men! You see, every one of us is accountable to God, so He has written us a love letter.

That letter (the Bible) tells you to beware of traditions (Colossians 2:8), and tells you what kind of church to join and serve in. It's important to study God's letter to gain insight into His exact plan for mankind and for you personally. Be faithful to God and His Book alone!

Next, beware of the "cults." There are a vast number of false prophets, many of whom are sincere and convinced that their sect is the only way. There are, for example, the Jehovah's Witnesses, the Mormons, the Christian Scientists, the Church of Scientology, and Spiritualism, to name a few. Some of the things they say sound good because they come from the Word, but they are out of context or misapplied. Other doctrines are manufactured from totally unrelated Scriptures and have evolved into another gospel. A good rule of thumb is this: when anyone says you need them or their church to get to Heaven, they are a false prophet. All we need is Christ! Never argue with a cult member. That would be counter-productive. Instead, you should know the truth well.

Last of all, there are the sound New Testament churches. You should look for one that is Biblical, Christ-centered, evangelistic, alive, and concerned. Pray that God will lead you to the one of His choice.

Can you answer the following questions about the local church?
1. Who thought up the idea of a "church?" *Matthew 16:18*

   _____

2. Does God expect you to be faithful to a church? *Hebrews 10:25*

   _____

3. Who is the head of a local church? *Ephesians 1:20-23; Ephesians 5:23*

   _____

4. When should you join a church? *Acts 2:41*

   _____

5. Should you join just any church?

   _____

6. What should you look for in a church home?

   _____

7. Do you have a New Testament, soul-winning, Gospel-preaching church home? If not, will you look for one?

   _____

Again, if your answer to the last question was "Yes," you are on the right path. "Faith comes by hearing and hearing by the Word of God" (Romans 10:17). A good, gospel-preaching church will enable your faith and your spiritual life to grow by leaps and bounds. There is still more to come, so let's see what it is!

LESSON 3

To Give or Not to Give

Stewardship

If the subject of baptism is one of the most controversial questions in Christianity, then the topic of stewardship is one of the most sensitive. In other words, this subject often needlessly offends people. That is proof of Satan's activity because stewardship is designed for us and our benefit, not for our detriment.

A pastor should never confront any member of the congregation—exceptions would be staff, teachers, and leaders—for the purpose of questioning them about their giving. It is between them and God, not them and the pastor. But, whether or not you are faithful in stewardship should in no way affect a change in your pastor's preaching or practice.

Tithing—the practice of giving 10% of one's gross income—was mentioned before the law was ever given to Moses (Genesis 14:18-20; 28:22). It was also part of the Mosaic Law (Leviticus 27:30-32; Malachi 3:10). Finally, it is mentioned specifically by Christ in the New Testament (Matthew 23:23). Paul indicated that, if anything, our giving ought to be more liberal than that commanded under the law, because we are under grace (1 Corinthians 16:2; 2 Corinthians 9:6-7)! He definitely teaches proportionate giving. After all, what is tithing? It is proportionate—10%—giving!

Tithing is equitable. God asks no more, and no less from the poor than He does from the rich. It is His program, and He personally blesses and rewards those who practice this teaching (Malachi 3:8-12; Luke 6:38; Acts 20:35; Matthew 6:19-21). The tithes and offerings are to be the "first fruits." God is our preferred creditor, and we should pay Him first (Proverbs 3:9-10; Malachi 3:8-12). They should be brought to the local New Testament church or storehouse (I Corinthians 16:2; Malachi 3:8-9; Deuteronomy 12:5-6, 11).

The tithe should not be sent to television or radio pastors, etc. These pastors may be sent gifts, but the tithe is supposed to be taken to the storehouse (the church). If we do not actively tithe, we are, in fact, saying that we know more than God does. He says it is best for us to do so, and we say that we can make it better by keeping and spending the tithe. We are, in fact, calling Him a liar. Further, we are saying we do not want Him as our partner. If this were not bad enough, we are showing that we do not love Him because He said, "If ye love Me, keep My commandments" (John 14:15). Last of all, we become common thieves (Malachi 3:8)! God wants us to give, so that we can receive, so we can give some more.

Critics in this church age, or age of grace, say that tithing is not for us. Frankly, I stopped tithing years ago! Instead, our household consistently gives more than a tithe to our local church. Our church receives between 10-13% of the incomes of many of our people. This is without coercion, threat, brow-beating, or shaming. They give because they want to do so cheerfully!

In addition to the giving of tithes and offerings for missions, building funds, schools, and operating expenses, we recognize the personal obligation to give to the needy and poor. What a joy to learn that while "getting" does not satisfy, "giving" does. Tithing is one of the hardest principles of Christianity to begin practicing, but often becomes the source of real joy and faith-building later on. Try it—you'll like it! In practicing stewardship, we ought to obey Luke 6:38 and learn to give by faith first, then allow God to bless us. A farmer doesn't reap a harvest until he first plants his fields. The same is true for the Christian. It has also been said to "give until it hurts." I believe we should give until it feels good! The old saying, "you can't out-give God," is still true. Try it and see if it won't work for you (Malachi 3:10).

Here are some good questions concerning stewardship:

1. What is God's plan for financing His work? Is it bingo, rummage sales, etc.?

2. Since God does command tithing and giving, and promises to bless you for it, will He keep His end of the promise? Can God lie? *Titus 1:2*

3. Do you need God as your "partner" in your financial dealings?

4. John 14:23 tells us if we love Him to keep His words (commands). Do you love God?

5. Are you guilty of robbery? *Malachi 3:8-9*

6. Do you presently tithe and give offerings? If not, will you begin to do so?

Things we ought to give as good stewards.

Self: *Romans 12:1*

Songs: *Hebrews 13:15*

Service: *Hebrews 13:16; Matthew 20:18; Romans 9:12*

Substance: *Hebrews 13:16*

Time: *Psalm 90:12; 2 Corinthians 5:10; Ephesians 5:16*

Talents: (abilities or gifts) the principle of *Matthew 25:14*

How should we give these things?

Liberally: *Proverbs 11:25; Luke 6:38*

Sacrificially: *2 Samuel 24:24*

Faithfully: *1 Corinthians 16:1-2* (You shall reap what you sow)

Expectantly: *Malachi 3:8-12; Luke 6:38* (knowing God will bless us for our faithfulness)

Cheerfully: *2 Corinthians 9:7; Exodus 25:2*

LESSON 4

Now Hear This!

Witnessing

We are saved to serve. We are commissioned by God (John 20:21; Matthew 28:18-20; Acts1:8) to go into the whole world telling others what Jesus means to us and what He can do for them. To be effective:

1) We must be convinced ourselves. All doubts about our salvation must be eliminated. Such Scriptures as I John 5:13; John 3:35-36; Romans 10:13, and many others will be helpful in understanding that God saves us eternally and that we can entrust ourselves to His keeping (see outline in back of this book "19 Reasons Why a Christian Can't be Lost!").

2) We must have a clear system of telling others the Good News.

The Roman's Road Plan of Salvation

We are all sinners (Romans 3:10). We are all lost (Romans 3:23). In your present sinful condition, you will spend eternity in hell (Romans 6:23). God loves us (Romans 5:8, John 3:16). You can be saved now (Romans 10:9-10, 13). You can know you are saved (1 John 5:13, John 3:36).

The scriptural plan for telling others is family first (Acts 1:8; John 1:40-42. Your "Jerusalem" is your immediate family and friends. "Judea" is that group of folks not quite as close as the first, and "Samaria" would be those not immediately thought of as genuine friends or acquaintances. Then, of course, the "uttermost parts" is the entire world. Witnessing is a personal thing done face to face between individuals. It's as simple as that—and yet it is all-encompassing as a worldwide missionary endeavor!

Did you realize it would be possible to evangelize the whole world in one generation if all Christians would be faithful? Figure it out for yourself. If we started with one person who would win just one other person to Christ this year, and if those two would win just two more next year, and if those four would win only four more the third year, etc; do you realize that in just 33 years, over six billion people would be saved?! In the 34th year, the rest of the world would be won! That is the New Testament plan. Isn't that exciting? Well, then, let's do it!

Here are some questions on witnessing:

1. Are you important in God's program of witnessing?
   _____

2. What are some Scriptures you can use in personal soul-winning or witnessing?
   _____

3. What is your personal testimony?
   a. What was your life like before you received Christ?

   b. What brought you to the realization of a need for Christ?

   c. When did you become a Christian?

   d. Who helped you with this decision?

   e. Did someone lead you to Christ in your home? If not, where?

   f. What does being a Christian mean to you and your family?

4. Are you willing to share the above with family, friends, and even those whom you have never met before? *Matthew 10:32*

5. List the names of some people to whom you would like to witness to immediately.

   1. _____ 2. _____
   3. _____ 4. _____
   5. _____ 6. _____
   7. _____ 8. _____
   9. _____ 10. _____

6. Would you be willing to participate in an assimilation system, following up with people who visit your church?

   _____

7. Can you find a Bible verse that promises God's blessings on soul-winning efforts?

   _____

LESSON 5

Operation Communication

Prayer and Bible Reading

There are literally thousands of books and study guides already written on how to pray and read the Bible. Why, then, are so many Christians still in the dark about how they are supposed to communicate with God? I think it is because quite often we try to make things harder than they actually are. Do you know what prayer really is? It is simply talking to God. Now you can talk, can't you? Of course you can! Then talk to God. Don't worry about not being able to pray this way, "Oh, Lord, God of Abraham, Isaac, Jacob and Joseph, the Great I AM, the Alpha and Omega, etc." Just talk to God

the way you would to your spouse or parents. On second thought, maybe that is part of your problem! Talk to Him more, and you will talk to *them* better! What kind of home would you have if you never spoke to anyone? Well, then, what kind of relationship can you have with God if you never speak to Him?

Prayer is talking with God while

Drawing near to Him *Hebrews 10:22; James 4:8; Psalm 73:28*

Giving thanks *Psalm 100:4*

Making intercession *1 Timothy 2:1*

Asking, seeking, and knocking *Matthew 7:7-8*

Anyone may pray. The righteous are encouraged to do so (James 5:16; Proverbs 15:8). Sinners are encouraged to do so (Luke 18:13). In fact, the most important thing a person can do is pray as a sinner and ask Jesus Christ to save him. We ought to pray for ourselves (Matthew 6:11-12), for the sick (James 5:15), and even for our enemies (Matthew 5:44).

When and where should we pray? Privately (Matthew 6:6), in church (Matthew 21:13), and frequently (Psalm 55:17). You need to be in an attitude of prayer all the time (1 Thessalonians 5:17). You don't have to close your eyes necessarily—especially while you are driving! You can pray while you are washing dishes, riding a bike, or walking the dog. The main thing is to make sure that you do it.

Learning to talk to someone is only half of what is necessary for communication to take place. If only one person speaks, it is a monologue, not a dialogue. No communication is complete without two sides. For example, how would it be if in a marriage the wife did all the talking? (Oops, bad example again!) "But how can I know what God is saying? Do I hear Him speak in an audible voice?" you may ask. No! But, we can hear His very words. Guess how? By reading the Bible. That's right. The Bible is God's Holy, inspired Word. It is a supernatural book inspired by a Supernatural Power, and it accomplishes supernatural results. God used over 40 human authors in the recording of His very words. These men wrote in great detail without any corroboration whatsoever. Many of them lived over one thousand years apart, and yet their prophecies and reports complement each other totally and accurately. The finished result is the infallible Word of Almighty God (2 Timothy 3:16; 2 Peter 1:21). We are to search it (John 5:39), delight in it (Psalm 119:16), and live it (James 1:25).

A helpful acrostic to help study the Scriptures:
- **S** Systematically *Luke 24:27*
- **E** Every day *Acts 17:11*
- **A** Ask God's help *Psalm 119:18*
- **R** Reverently *Psalm 119:172*
- **C** Carefully *Psalm 119:1-2, 4*
- **H** Hide it in your heart *Psalm 119:11*

Naturally, you will not understand all of the Bible the first time through. It is, after all, an infinite mind communicating with finite people. The point is, as we study, the Holy Spirit helps us and teaches us from the holy pages. Many things come to us in the pages of Scripture: wisdom, understanding, and even faith (Proverbs 3:4-6; Romans 10:17). I hope you see now how important it is to communicate with your God. What power we can have if only we will do what He has commanded! Know what the Bible teaches about Jesus Christ and salvation by grace through faith. A bank teller does not learn to detect counterfeit money by handling bogus bills, but rather by handling only good money. When the false dollar turns up, then he/she knows instantly! There is no need to study in depth all the views of other cults. Instead, just know the truth so you can effectively witness to those who are clinging to a baptism, a man, or whatever for salvation.

Let's answer some more questions:

1. Who wrote the Bible?

2. How often should you read it?

3. What will reading the Bible do for you?

4. If men wrote the Bible, doesn't it contain error?

5. Will you vow to read God's Word at least 5 minutes every single day without exception? (Make sure you intend to do it if you make this vow to God!)

6. What is prayer?

7. What if you don't know how to pray?

8. Who should pray?

9. Is there anything too little or too big with which to bother God through prayer?

10. Will you pray every day (several times) to God?

   If so, proceed to the next lesson. If not, better repeat this lesson.

LESSON 6

Growing Pains

Problems

Congratulations! Now that you're a Christian—a born-again child of God—you're perfect, right? Wrong! If you think you are perfect now, just ask your husband, wife or parents—as the case may be. They will tell you in short order! NO, the fact is, we are not perfect even though we want to be. We should, however, live as perfectly as we can and then one day when we're with Him, we will be perfect. But, as long as we are in this life, we will fall short. This fact gives rise to a great and terrible error in the theology of many Christians. It is often taught that if you sin too much, you are no longer saved. Let me use the illustration that Jesus used to disprove that teaching. In John 3:3, 5, we read these amazing words, "You must be born again…." Now, all of us were born the first time physically. We have physical life, a physical birth, and physical parents. However,

Jesus has said that this is not enough to be able to see heaven. We must be born again. Does that mean we need to be baptized? Join a church? Give money? No! We do not have to do these things to get to heaven. We ought to do them because we are going there. There is a great difference. We simply must experience a spiritual birth to have spiritual life and a spiritual parent —God the Father.

After we have done this—accepted Christ as our personal Savior and Lord—(Romans 10:9-10, 13), can we ever be unborn spiritually or lost again? Well, can you ever be unborn physically? You say, "Of course not." I contest earnestly, therefore, that as a child of God, we can not lose our salvation. Instead, if we're disobedient, God will discipline us (Hebrews 12:5-13). If you are a parent and your children disobey you—if they ever do—they are still your children. If they rebel, run away from home, or change their names, it makes no difference. They are still your children. When children disobey, the Bible tells us we are to discipline them in love. That's what God does for us. He disciplines us in love. Your spiritual birth, then, is just as irreversible as your physical birth. John 3:36 says, "He that believes on the Son has—present tense—everlasting life…." Now, let me ask you another question: What is everlasting life? Simply stated, it is life without end; and if we have trusted Christ, we have that commodity—"everlasting life." Does it end next week? No! Next month? No! Then, does it end when you sin? The answer is again no! If it did stop, it would not be "everlasting." It would have to be called something else like "temporary life" or "spiritual life," etc. Sin breaks fellowship with God, but not the relationship.

I hope you realize that when you do fall—like a baby just learning to take his first steps—you need to get up again, dust yourself off (I John 1:9), and try harder with God's help (Philippians 4:13). Don't expect to be perfect, but try to be as perfect as you can. I'm reminded of a sticker I've seen on cars lately. It says, "Christians aren't perfect, just forgiven." Trust God to lead you to a better life. Trust Him to forgive you when you sin. Some other verses of encouragement might be: Romans 8:35-39; 1 Peter 1:3-6; Jude 24-25; Psalm 51.

Oh yes, think about this. If Jesus Christ is real, so is Satan. The same Bible teaches about both of them. You will soon learn that your greatest enemies are the world—the present anti-God system, the flesh—self, and the devil, (1 John 2:16). Just remember that the Bible teaches, "Greater is He that is in you than he that is in the world" (1 John 4:4). Be well acquainted with our defense as outlined in Ephesians 6:11-18. Seek to be Spirit-controlled and respond to trials in the correct manner. The Christian life is the greatest there is! Though upsets may come, we know Who is at the controls, and that makes it worth it all!

Now see if you can answer these questions:

1. If you sin after you've received Christ, are you lost again?

2. Does this mean you can sin all you want after you're saved, without any consequences?

3. What will happen when you do disobey your Father?

4. Who saved you? Then, who is the only One that can keep you saved?

5. What is a good verse to claim after you have sinned and want to ask God's forgiveness?

6. Who and what do you need to be on the lookout for, lest they trip you up in your spiritual walk? (Three categories)

7. Why do we have trials and testing?

8. What does it mean to be Spirit-controlled? Are you being Spirit-controlled? If not, will you be?

Spiritual Growth Chart

Name _____

Date of Birth _____

Place of Birth _____

Date of "New Birth" _____

Place of "New Birth" _____

Date of Baptism _____

Place of Baptism _____

Baptized by _____

Church Membership _____

Pastor _____

Date Joined _____

Date Began Tithing _____

People I need to tell about Christ:

_____

_____

_____

_____

_____

LESSON 7

Follow the Leader

The Holy Spirit

The Holy Spirit is our leader. God gives Him to us to teach us, comfort us, bring God's Word to remembrance, and to empower us to live above our sinful natures. He is necessary if we're to be in service for God, have power to live and have victory over and deliverance from sin. Lately, there's been an abundance of talk about the Holy Spirit, Who, by the way, is a personal Being, not a nondescript vapor effusing the universe. Much of what you may hear is not based on the truth of the Gospel. I encourage you to make a personal study of God's Holy Spirit so that you may know the truth.

Practical steps to knowing you are filled with the Holy Spirit:

1) **Accept Jesus Christ as your personal Savior.**
   The Holy Spirit will always draw people to Jesus and NOT to Himself.

2) **Change your mind about sin – repent!**
   Anything that stands between you and God becomes sin and will keep you from being "filled" with the Holy Spirit. Beware of even those so-called "small" sins.

3) **Make an open confession of salvation to the world!**
   Upon receiving Christ, be baptized by immersion immediately and publicly. You cannot be a Spirit-filled Christian and a secret one, too! If you've been saved, but not baptized, you cannot be Spirit-filled, because you're not being obedient to God's Word.

4) **Give yourself an unconditional surrender to the Holy Spirit.**
Acts 5:32 says; the Holy Spirit always draws people to Jesus and NOT to Himself. "We are witnesses of these things; and so is the Holy Spirit, whom God hath given to them that obey Him." We must give ourselves in unconditional surrender to God. We cannot just be obedient in a few things. We must be obedient in all things. Is there something so important that it would keep us from the fullness of God's blessed Holy Spirit?

5) **Thirst after the Holy Spirit.**
In other words, make God your most important need. As a man dying of thirst would cry out for "Water!" determine within yourself, "I MUST have God's power in my life!"

6) **Ask to be filled with the Holy Spirit.**
Ask God to fill you with His Holy Spirit. Luke 11:13 says, "If you then, being evil, know how to give good gifts unto your children: how much more shall your heavenly Father give the Holy Spirit to them that ask Him!" Pray a DEFINITE prayer for a DEFINITE answer.

7) **Believe God's Promise.**
   Exercise faith. Mark 11:24 says, "...I say unto you, what things soever you desire, when you pray, believe that you receive them, and you shall have them." And James said, "...but let him ask in faith nothing wavering." Yes, you can be filled by the Holy Spirit and used of God in a mighty and wonderful way. As a matter of fact, God's Word says He is looking for men and women who will be willing to conform to His Word so that they may be blessed with power from on high. I hope you will determine right now to be a "super-natural" Christian!

Here are some questions to help us "Follow the Leader:"

1. The Holy Spirit is a person. Are you prepared to make HIM the leader of your life?

2. The Holy Spirit is given to us by God the Father. His purpose is to do the following things for us:

3. Anything that stands between you and God is called:

4. God gives his Spirit to those who _____ Him.

5. If you want to be filled with the Holy Spirit, you must be willing to pray and ask for filling. Are you willing to forsake known sin and ask to be filled with the Holy Spirit?

6. When you pray, you must _____. Believing God makes Him happy and allows Him to answer prayers.

7. Is it true that God wants to use you in His service?

   Yes, God wants YOU. You can be used by Him if you're willing to be obedient and a fit vessel for His Holy Spirit.

BEGIN A CLOSER WALK WITH CHRIST

19 Reasons Why A Christian Cannot Be Lost

I Have Been Chosen

This was before the foundation of the world (Ephesians 1:4). Why would God choose me before the foundation of the world if I were to be lost again? Isn't Christ omniscient and doesn't He know all? If I could be lost again, His choice was poor.

God's Foreknowledge About Me

God's Word says, He knew, or foreknew, that I would be saved (Romans 8:29). If God foreknew I was going to be saved, why not that I would backslide and be lost? If He foreknew my salvation, why not my backsliding? It is reasonable to ask, "If He knew I would backslide, why did He save me in the first place?" Surely the Lord foreknew what I would do before He saved me. His foreknowledge of my failure afterward did not stop Him from saving me.

I Am Predestinated

I was predestinated to be saved (Ephesians 1:5).

A. God foreknew I would be saved.

B. Because He foreknew, I was predestinated (Romans 8:29).

C. Because I was called, I was justified (Romans 8:30).

D. Because I was justified, I was glorified. This is according to the foreknowledge of God. If a Christian can be lost again, then God's foreknowledge is no good, for His Word says that God's foreknowledge saw the Christian even glorified.

I Am Born Again
A Christian has been "born again, born from above" (John 3:5-6). He has been "born of God" (1 John 5:1). If a Christian is born, may he be unborn? It is impossible to be "unborn;" therefore, it is not possible to be lost from above.

I Have Eternal Life (A Present Possession)
Every Christian is given eternal life by Christ. "I give unto them eternal life." (John 10:28). He now has this life (1 John 5:13). This life is not for ten, twenty, or thirty years, nor as long as we can hold out but it is for eternity…forever (John 6:47; John 5:24; John 3:36; I John 5:12-13). One cannot be lost when one has eternal life.

I Have A New Nature
Every Christian possesses a new nature (1 Peter 1:3-4), God's nature. If a Christian could be lost with such a nature, this would bring God down to a human level, and God's nature would be lost.

I Am The Temple Of The Holy Spirit

Every Christian is the temple of the Holy Spirit (1 Corinthians 6:19). He is sealed by the Spirit until the day of redemption (Ephesians 4:30). He is not sealed until he backslides, but "unto the day of redemption." The Holy Spirit abides in the Christian forever (John 14:16). If a Christian can be lost again, the Holy Spirit is also lost, for He abides in the Christian forever. John 14:16 clearly teaches us that the Holy Spirit will never leave the Christian. It is appropriate to ask, "Could the temple of the Holy Spirit go to a place called hell?"

In God's Sight, I Am Now In Heaven

God has raised us "with Christ;" that is, when Christ was raised from the grave, we were also raised. Our position as Christians is sealed together with Him in the heavenlies (Ephesians 2:5-6). We are now, as far as God is concerned, in heaven. If a Christian can be lost again, then he must be put out of heaven, since he now occupies that place (Colossians 3:3-4).

I Am Part Of Christ's Body

We, as Christians, are members of Christ's body – flesh of His flesh and bone of His bone (Ephesians 5:30). If a Christian can be lost again, then Christ is lost with him, since He made the Christian part of His own body. If he can be lost again, the body will not be complete, and if this is true, the plan and work of Christ is lost and useless—the Word of God speaks of Christ's body being "without spot or wrinkle" (Ephesians 5:25-27).

I Am Complete In Christ

Every Christian is now completed in Him (Colossians 2:10). Can the completed work of Christ be lost again? If it can be lost, was it ever complete? How can a Christian be complete and lost again? Wouldn't then the completed work of Christ go to hell?

I Am Saved By Grace

"For by grace are ye saved" (Ephesians 2:8-9; Acts 15:11). If a man is saved by grace, and grace is unmerited favor and wholly undeserved, how can he be lost? If he can be lost through some sin or by not being faithful, can it be said of him, "by grace are ye saved?" If our reaching heaven depends upon our good works, then our salvation would have no element of grace in it.

I Will Not Be Cast Out Again

John 6:37 teaches very clearly that it is the Christian who will never be cast out. The Christian is the Father's love gift to the Son, and Christ dares not discard those whom the Father gives Him.

I Have No Condemnation

The Child of God, according to Romans 8:1, will never come into condemnation nor judgment. Since his sins were judged at the cross of Calvary, we are assured in John 3:18 and John 5:24 that the believer is freed from condemnation. Christ bore the punishment of our sins. God cannot pour His judgment upon the believer if Christ bore the penalty of "all our sins."

I Am An Incorruptible Seed
Since the Christian has been born of incorruptible seed, can he be corrupt (1 Peter 1:23)? It is impossible. How can that which is incorruptible ever be corrupt?

Christ Will Finish What He Has Begun
He who began the work must finish it (Philippians 1:6). He cannot fail. If a Christian can be lost again, then Christ is unable to complete that which He started. Is anything too hard for God?

He Is Able To Keep Me
"He is able to keep that which I have committed unto Him against [or until] that day" (2 Timothy 1:12). He is able to keep one from falling (Jude 24). I am not expected to keep myself, for I am not able. He not only can keep me, but also keep that which I have committed unto Him until the day of redemption is complete.

I Am Preserved Forever
All His saints are preserved forever. They are preserved in Christ (Jude 1; Psalm 31:23).

Salvation Is A Gift To Me

"The gift of God is eternal life through Jesus Christ our Lord" (Romans 6:23). Do we earn a gift? If so, it is not a gift. One receives Christ (John 1:12; 1 John 5:12). One does not merit salvation. If he does nothing to deserve it, it is impossible to do anything to lose it.

Christ's Work For Me

He made peace for me (Colossians 1:20; Ephesians 2:15). Surely this peace is eternal peace. He forever put away my sins (Hebrews 9:26). It is, therefore, inconsistent to think that He will bring them up before me again. He bore my sins—past, present, and future (1 Peter 2:24). If Christ atoned for my sins—past, present, and future—are there any more for me to bear? The answer to that question is "no."